Thank you for coming

Gospel Reflections
by
Graham Jeffery

Palm Tree

Designed by Michael Green

© Copyright 1982 Graham Jeffery

PALM TREE PRESS LTD,
55 Leigh Road,
Leigh-on-Sea, Essex.

ISBN 0 86208 033 9

Printed by E.T. Heron, Essex & London.

It is hard to know where any gospel begins: with our Lord's birth in Bethlehem; or in Mary's heart; or in the events of Pentecost when Jesus came to life in his disciples, and was born a second time.

The reader, then, will forgive the chronology of this little book; as also the verses of scripture, which are not from any particular translation but are offered simply as pegs for other better minds to hang their coats upon.

Perhaps, also, the story of Jesus begins more surely with you who read this book, and follow Him, albeit in darkness, in your own life.

In any case, you will forgive my presumption in so 'meditating', and go on where I fall short, yet remember me a sinner.

GRAHAM JEFFERY
Pyecombe Rectory

Come to me all who labour and are heavy laden.
Matthew 11:28

My search for friends,
son, daughter,
is always a choice of sinners.
Your emptiness
and rough exterior
is all I ever need.

Mary said: 'I am the Lord's hand-maid.
Let it be according to your word.' Luke 1:38

'Amen' usually comes at the end
    of our prayers, Lord,
    of our attempts to follow you.
    But here, in Mary's verse,
    it's a beginning:
    not mumbled quietly
        at the end of a distant collect,
    but spoken clearly, for you alone.
        Amen.
        So let it be.
        So may he
            be born.

*. . . and laid him in a manger
because there was no room for them at the inn.* Luke 2:7

Your first pulpit still speaks to me, Lord:
its plain wood, and the child's cry inside it;
and even the inadequacies of your first congregation,
the straw and the bare earth.
All these remind me
that the awkward circumstances of my own temperament
are no barrier to your coming:
the wood and the straw of my life
are all you need to be born.

You will find the child wrapped in swaddling clothes and lying in a manger. Luke 2:12

I sometimes wonder, Lord,
how far you travelled
from this poor stable
      where you were born.
The donkey stayed with you,
appearing again
      as you rode into Jerusalem.
The wood of the crib
kept you company in the carpenter's shop,
and would be there,
along with the world's neglect,
      when you died on the cross.
And so, Lord,
      bearing this in mind,
I think I can see
your whole story,
   your whole love,
   on page one of your life.

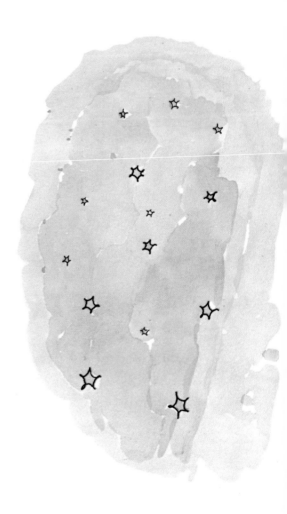

We have seen his star in the east . . . Matthew 2:2

It seems a funny place to start a gospel, Lord,
miles away in space,
far away from Jerusalem,
light years from Bethlehem.
With a star,
 squandered and burnt out
 by the time its light reached earth.
And yet, most of your servants, Lord,
 seem to have been the same:
 burnt out, dead and buried
 by the time their words
 were fully understood.
Yet, dying and neglected,
lonely and forgotten,
they point to you.
And they, especially,
 prepare your way.

The star . . . went before them. Matthew 2:9

I have sometimes wondered, Lord,
how you came to choose your star.
There are so many of them,
all seeming the same to me.
'When you have seen one star
you have seen the lot.'
And yet, Lord,
    each star has its own place
    in its own constellation,
    its own galaxy.
And you know them all by name.
      So does each soul
      have its own place,
      completing with its life
        all other souls,
        however many they may be.
          And all I ask
          is that I,
          who have my own place
          in so great a galaxy of human souls,
          may, by my life,
          assist at least one of them.

There came wise men from the east, to Jerusalem.
Matthew 2:1

That's what I like about you, Lord,
you begin as you mean to go on,
breaking down in your earliest days
the barriers and the distances
                    that separate us from each other,
                    that seem to separate us from you.
For distance is not only measured in miles, Lord.
It is our loneliness that separates us from each other,
making us strangers to the world.
Yet you, Lord,
        reach out your hand to touch us.
        You touched the leper, and that distance crumbled;
        you spoke to Mary, and her separation vanished away.
        So, as a baby to these foreign kings,
        you hold out your hand from the crib,
        beginning as you mean to go on.

*There was at that time a man in Jerusalem
named Simeon . . . He had been told by the Spirit
that he would not see death until he had seen
the Lord's Christ.* Luke 2:25, 26

I met you, Lord,
when my life was over
and I had no future to lay at your feet;
only inability, and the memory of things
            I could have done better.
            But you will understand, Lord,
            being at the beginning and end of every life.
            And I, who approach the end of things,
                look forward now
                to a longer acquaintance with you.

*Arise! Take the young child and his mother,
and flee to Egypt. Stay there till I tell you
it is safe.* Matthew 2:13

Travelling to Egypt,
one refugee in a world of refugees;
you will have no settled place, Lord,
where you can lay your head,
no one to understand you fully,
no life of ease.
Yet we, Lord,
    insecure as we are
    in faith or temperament,
    ask you, the journeying one,
    to travel with us.

*And Jesus went down with them to Nazareth,
and was obedient to them.* Luke 2:51

You seem to have spent all your life
at the carpenter's bench, Lord,
in one way or another:
carving the wood,
hammering the nails,

saying to your father:
"Look, Joseph, it is finished,
this table, this chair,
          which took me three hours to make."
And then, Lord,
when you left home
and the carpenter's shop behind,
you went on carving, went on working,
until at the end you could say:
"Look, Father,
     this other thing I made:
     it is finished.
     This life of mine,
     completed again with wood and nails,
     taking me thirty years to make.
     And for your sake I leave it,
     hoping it may be of use
          to those who come after."

There was a man from God, whose name was John.
John 1:6

Strictly, Lord,
John does not belong in your book.
He is not necessary,
    for he came
        six months before;
        in his birth,
        in his public life and preaching,
        even in his death,
           he was not all that far
               ahead of you.
           And yet, we all need signposts,
           arrows pointing,
           lives to prepare your life,
               your coming.

When the Jews sent messengers to ask him
who he was, John confessed: 'I am not the Christ.
' John 1:19, 20

I did not ask to be remembered, Lord.
I did not ask for a place in this book,
                or your life.
Not even to be one of your children,
                    one of your disciples.
For I, Lord,
            could not carry on
                    your work or life.
            I could only point:
                a voice proclaiming,
                a signpost directing.
            "No, not me.
            No, not my words,
                my life,
            for I am not anything
                or anyone at all.
                Simply a voice
                    leading to you."

A voice from heaven said:
'This is my beloved son, in whom I am well pleased.'
Matthew 3:17

Do you remember your ordination, Lord?
I suppose you would,
for a wet time you had of it,
with John baptising you,
and your Father's voice easy to hear.
But now, Lord,
the voice is not so clear,
with yourself on Calvary,
and the voices of the soldiers
crowding out any others.
Yet now, Lord, especially,
do you comfort us
     who have grown old in your service,
     duller . . . perhaps.
     For the voice we heard then
     so clearly at our first starting out,
     will return to comfort us
          at our departing.

The tempter came to him: 'If you are the Son of God, tell these stones to become bread.' Matthew 4:3

As things are, they are.
The stones remained stones for you, Lord,
as they do for us.
And, though we long for change,
the hardness of this world
does not seem to alter.
The stones are still stones
when you come out of the wilderness,
not bread to eat;
and if you fall on them
no angels will hold you up.
And yet, Lord,
we who face the hardness of this world
and long for change
when the stones remain hard,
now have this consolation:
As we are, so are you in the world.

*Is not this Joseph's son? We know his father
and mother.* John 6:42

It's nice to be one of a family, Lord.
Not all of us manage it.
But you did, being fortunate
                    in your parents.
But you did not leave it there, Lord:
calling Peter, James and John your brothers,
Magdalene your sister,
and all of us,
     your own dear children.
So you, Lord,
who call all the world your family
will, if you have your way,
                  lose not one.

Jesus went into the Synagogue on the Sabbath day.
It was his turn to read the lesson, and
the reading was from Isaiah:

> *'The Spirit of the Lord is upon me,*
> *because he has sent me*
> *to announce good news to the poor,*
> *to proclaim the prisoners' release,*
> *and sight to those who are blind;*
> *to let the broken victims go free,*
> *to proclaim a year of the Lord's favour.'*
> *When he had finished reading, he rolled*
> *up the scroll and began to speak: 'Today,*
> *in your very hearing, this verse has come*
> *true.'* Luke 4:16-21

You did not come to dose us with religion, Lord,
you came to bring us life.
In you, love of God and love of neighbour
came off the tablets,

> long venerated,
> took arms and legs,
> and walked among us.
> Not another commandment,
> but the old ones brought to life,
> lived in you, for the first time.
> No need any longer for 'religion'.

The first thing Andrew did was to find his brother . . .
John 1:41

Lord,
    do you still remember Andrew?
    He would understand if you didn't.
    He being
        the smaller of the two brothers,
        the one you did *not* call your 'rock',
        the one who did not go with you
            and see you transfigured.
    And yet, Lord,
        it was he who brought the two of you together
        saying to Peter: "I have found the Christ",
        bringing him to you,
        giving you your chief disciple;

as he did later
    with that small boy
    and his inadequate picnic.
Again Andrew would stand back,
and having introduced a miracle,
ask no more than that,
    to be your servant,
    watch the gifts of others
    grow in your hands,
    the small become many,
    the weak and diffident become plentiful.
And yet, Lord,
    if he does that
    Andrew is indeed
    the chief of all apostles:
    the man the world ignores, as it passes by,
    following *his* directions to you.

Follow me. Matthew 4:19

I wish you had come later, Lord,
then I too could have left my nets
            and followed you,
hearing you speak, seeing you live,
sharing my life with you;
denying you, and making the same mistakes,
only to see you rise again.
But then, Lord,
        you do come
            in the same way,
            with the same voice speaking to us,
            the same life given to us to share.

32

There was a wedding in Cana of Galilee . . .
and they ran out of wine. John 2:1

We carry this treasure, Lord,
    in earthen vessels:
    six plain water-pots of stone,
    used only to carrying
    the most ordinary water.
    Twelve disciples,
    used only to carrying
    the plainest of friendships,
    the most ordinary of lives,
    And ourselves also,
    awkward
        and quite unsuited
        to the difficulties of discipleship.
    And yet, Lord,
    it is always us,
      the empty ones,
      the inadequate ones,
      that you bless,
        and use.

When the master of ceremonies tasted the water
that had been turned into wine he said:
'You have kept the best wine til now.' John 2:9,10

I did not ask to be filled with wine, Lord.
    Ordinary water will be enough.
    Though I long sometimes
    for a more exciting life,
        a more illustrious position,
        a better relationship with my children,
        an easier relationship with myself.

And yet,
　　　being filled with this plain water, Lord,
　　　I only ask that you pass
　　　your hand over it,
　　　changing its contents,
　　　with all their inadequacy,
　　　　　into your wine.

Jesus said: 'Lazarus, come forth', and he did so,
still dressed in his white winding cloth. John 11:43, 44

Funny you told this story twice, Lord,
      but then I suppose you wanted us to know
      this resurrection of yours,
          with its empty tomb,
          and the stone rolled away,
          and all hope apparently gone,
          is our resurrection
             as well as yours.
          You are not the only one to rise from the dead.
          Lazarus does.
             We all do.
          In our hearts also
             you roll back the stone,
                and are alive.

*Zacchaeus, being a little man, could not see Jesus
for the crowd. So he ran on ahead and climbed a
sycamore tree.* Luke 19:3,4

I don't know whether I am coming or going, Lord,
but with you I seem to be both!
Coming to you, just as I am,
with all the disadvantages of my position;
and going with you,
my very weaknesses
       turned to strength.
        For if I am your disciple, Lord,
           there is hope for *all* your children.

*Be quick and come down. I want to dine
at your house today.* Luke 19:5

I'm a small man, Lord,
in more ways than one,
always needing other people's approval
      to give me meaning,
        to secure me a place in society.
        But when I met you, Lord,
        your love held me up.
        Standing on your shoulders
        I was small no longer.
        No need for sycamores now.

39

Peter said: 'If it is you, Lord, bid me
come to you over the water.' Matthew 14:28

It is easy to get out of the boat, Lord,
and perhaps I did it too easily,
setting out to follow you
        all those years ago
        when your voice came clearly to me
            across the water.
        But then the waves rose higher
        and I was overwhelmed by events,
        not hearing you,
        not seeing you clearly.
        Then, Lord, I cried to you again,
        in desperation, not confidence,
            this second time.
        And you, always with me,
          held me up.

Jesus said: 'Come'. Matthew 14:29

Starting anything is difficult, Lord:
getting out of the boat,
leaving behind the familiar smells,
the nets in place,
and all the companions of my former life.
And when I had done so, Lord,
it did not seem any easier;
and when it was too late to go back
I found myself drowning
       between two lives:
       the one I had tried to leave,
       the one I was trying to follow.
And yet, Lord,
    all our life is spent here
    in this land of no-between,
      this difficulty of being
       what I want to be.
     And you, who love me in this situation now,
       stretch out your hand.

But when he saw the strength of the waves
he began to sink. Matthew 14:30

We have to look at the world, Lord;
it would be irresponsible not to:
the difficulties which seem to overwhelm us,
the waves getting higher and higher,
and underneath us
             the frail circumstances and events
             which cannot support us.
        Yet, Lord,
        even if these things
        do stop us looking at you,
        we still cry to you in desperation;
             and our need is enough.

Lord, save me. Matthew 14:30

For a moment, Lord,
all went well
as I started out,
leaving the security of my family's boat,
going to you across the water.
But then I lost heart,
the waves rising higher,
and the fishing boat—so longed for—
                    beyond recall.
Then, Lord, in desperation I cried to you,
not looking to you now, except in fear.
And you, whom I followed so easily,
          so thoughtlessly before,
             were there to hold me.

Were not ten cleansed? Where are the nine?
Only this stranger has come back to give thanks to God.
Luke 17:17

One out of ten, Lord,
is not a very good score.
But at least you got more for healing:
>   ten out of ten for lepers cleansed,
>   ten out of ten for Magdalene accepted,
>   ten out of ten for Zacchaeus loved,
>   and ten out of ten for loving me.

Jesus took her by the hand and said . . . 'Get up'.
And at once the little girl got up and walked.
Mark 5:41

I wish you would do it again, Lord:
take your church by the hand,
take your world by the hand,
and raise her to new life,
and say to those who mourn:
        "She is not dead but asleep".
        But since, Lord,
           'church' and 'world' are big words,
                big matters,
        perhaps you would begin
           by raising me.

And there arose a great storm.
Waves burst into the ship. Mark 4:37

I get so worked up, Lord;
there are storms inside me,
as well as outside;
difficulties, unfaced decisions,
past failures,
things I should have done,
                    but somehow avoided.
All these conspire together
            to make a raging storm
            I cannot quell.
But you, who are with me
            in my failures,
                understand my difficulties,
                    and give me peace.

*Jesus took the bread and blessed it,
and gave it to the people.* John 6:11

I felt so inadequate, Lord,
standing there, with my five loaves
                and two small fish.
And yet you said to me:
        "It is enough".
        This character,
        this temperament,
        this situation in life,
        is all you ever need.

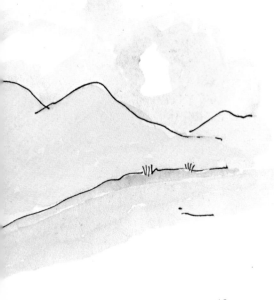

Now there was plenty of grass there,
so the people sat down. John 6:10

I'm glad you noticed the grass, Lord.
It seemed the only thing in your favour,
except for the small boy
       and his inadequate picnic,
       and Peter, James and John,
       and your other friends.
       But you took what you had, Lord,
       and gave thanks for it all;
       so that even the weaknesses of my own life
       seem, after this sign,
           enough to feed a world.

And there was a woman who had had a flow of blood for twelve years . . . Mark 5:25

They say time is a great healer, Lord.
> It can settle things
> in other ways too;
> illnesses, or states of mind,
>> or just failures.
> After twelve years
> these things are part of you.
> My illness and I
>> are become inseparable.
> But you separated them at once, Lord,
> seeing me for myself,
>> behind the illness,
> letting me touch you;
> you yourself touching me.
> And releasing my illness from me
>> for ever.

A woman who had suffered from a flow of blood for twelve years said to herself: 'If I touch even his clothes I shall be cured'. Mark 5:25, 28

We all need protection
 —from the world,
 from other people,
 from things that hurt us, Lord.
 We need to know where our life ends
 and other people's begin.
 Building fences to protect ourselves,
 we say without meaning to:
 'Thus far shall you come, and no further'.
 But you had no fences around your life, Lord,
 no signs saying 'Keep out. No entry'.
 Whoever touched the outside of your life,
    even the edge of your cloak,
    was noticed and welcomed.
  And we,
   who come with illness or habits of life,
   so ingrained as to be part of us,
   touch the very outside of your cloak,
    and are made well.

There was once a rich man who dressed in purple and
fine linen, and feasted in great magnificence every day.
At his gate, covered with sores, lay a poor man . . .
Luke 16:19,20

It is funny how blind I am, Lord,
and I became so gradually.
This unusual form of blindness
allows me

> to see
> distant objects,
> and people I look forward to meeting,
> while those on my own doorstep
>> I hardly notice.
>> Seeing them every day
>> they become so much part
>>> of my mental landscape
>> as to be invisible;
>> and the six or seven yards
>> which separates them from me every morning
>> becomes the longest distance in the world.

But when, Lord,
> I realise
>> it is you sitting there at my gate,
>> greeting me, in your poverty of ideas,
>> in your lack of social graces,
>>> I stop.
>> And as I stretch out one hand to you,
>>> or spare one thought,
>>> if only for a second,
>>> the longest distance in the world
>>>> becomes the shortest.

John in prison heard what Christ was doing,
and sent his own disciples to ask: 'Are you he that
should come, or are we still looking for another?'
Matthew 11:2, 3

The only sunlight some people have, Lord,
is the feeling
that at least
     they were right in choosing you.
     When even that comfort is taken away,
     as it is from John,
     their darkness seems complete.
     But you send your message, Lord:
          the blind see,
          the poor are fed,
          and we also, who see no light at all,
          have the good news told to us.

Are not two sparrows sold for a farthing? Yet not one of them falls to the ground without your Father.
Matthew 10:29

Lord, you will have noticed us,
    the two of us together,
    only fetching one farthing,
    the smallest coin
    in man's currency.
    But in your currency, Lord,
    we do rather better.
    You have a special place for us,
        the little coins,
        the little animals,
        the little things,
        the little people.
    And so, Lord,
    knowing you are listening,
    we praise you in the morning.

*A man was on his way from Jerusalem to Jericho,
and fell among thieves.* Luke 10:30

Some people make a mess of their journey, Lord.
   I think I was one of those,
   setting off when I was advised not to,
   finding the journey too much for me,
   and left by its difficulties
   half dead, unable to go on.
   But then you came,
   stopping your life to take care of me,
   and putting me on your own beast,
   yourself walking beside me.
   That has always been our relationship, Lord.
      It always will be.

A priest happened to be passing, but when he saw him he went by on the other side. Luke 10:31

Ah'm, Lord!
I think I missed an opportunity.
For though I saw you there,
and went back later,
     you had gone.
     So I travel on,
          treading the deep rivulets of this 'other side',
                well trodden
                and filled with traffic.
          And yet I long sometimes
                to swing my vehicle over,
                     move my life to your side of the road
                          where the poor lie waiting.

But a certain Samaritan came upon him,
and was moved to pity. Luke 10:33

Who owns the Jericho road, Lord?
Whose responsibility is it, anyway?
You'd have thought they would have improved it,
     made it more safe for traffic,
     done something about
          this breakdown in law and order.
But when I saw this donkey stop
and noticed the concern on one traveller's face
     —looking for bandages,
     pouring out oil and wine,
     giving up the use of his own donkey—
I realised then
          whose road it really was,
          and never again asked
          why *they* did nothing about it.
          For after all, Lord,
               this road is my responsibility now.
                    You have given the care of it to me.

A certain man had two sons. The younger came to him and said: 'Give me my share of the inheritance now'. Then he went to a far country and squandered it all in riotous living . . . When he came to himself he said: 'I know what I shall do. I will go back and return to my father'. Luke 15:11-13, 18

As soon as I even thought of you
   this rough path
      became part of the way home;
      and even my failures
      and lost opportunities,
      as I came back
      became part of your kindness to me:
         a sign of your love.

It would have been nice
to come back with something, Lord,
    but I had nothing to show
    for my time away.
    All you had given me
    I'd lost,
        the money gone,
        gifts and opportunities wasted.
        All I had
            as I came back
            was the dull failure of my past,
            and a longing for home.
And yet, more than gifts of frankincense,
        these touch your heart,
            and my empty-handedness is enough.

When he was yet a great way off, his father saw him.
Luke 15:20

I didn't know God was bald, Lord,
      short of breath,
      forgetting to put on his jacket
      and only wearing braces
      in his hurry to get up the road.
I didn't know he had false teeth,
    and that a bad heart condition
    had made him retire early,
    leaving most of the work to the elder son
        he obviously adored.
And yet, as I see him
      waiting so long, with an eye fixed
      on the distant hill where he'd last seen
        his other son,
      an ear listening all these years
      for his other son's footsteps on the drive outside,
      I seem to hear,
        not just the puffing and panting
        of one old man,
        but the love of God himself.

The elder son was out in the fields.
When he heard the music and dancing he refused to go in.
Luke 15:25.28

I was the one who stayed at home, Lord,
    never strayed far away,
    never, perhaps, risked anything,
    being partly dutiful, partly afraid,
    never knowing what it is like
    to see the old family home
    from a distance, in perspective,
    never seeing your dear figure
    running towards me, arms outstretched,
    as if my return
    were the only thing that mattered in the world,
    that I should be
    sure of your love.
    And ready with you
        to welcome my brother
        when he returns.

Each day has troubles enough of its own.
Matthew 6:34

Lord, I ask your blessing
        on this moment only.
        Nothing else.
        Yesterday is past,
        though I often regret it.
        Tomorrow will come,
        and I'm often afraid of it.
        But this moment only
            can I influence
            in any way.
            And I need
                your help
                    to do it.

I am come to set fire to the earth.
Luke 12:49

I'm surprised at your choice of kindling, Lord.
It is not what
        I would have chosen
        to set the world on fire,
        and light up our hearts for ever.
        But you laid the fire
        with twelve poor fishermen,
        then drenched all its hope with your death.
        Yet, Lord,
        this poor drenched bonfire
        burst into flame.
        And our own hearts,
        poor and inadequate,
        still wait for your kindling.

When he came in sight of the city, he wept over it.
Luke 19:41

This trickle of tears,
a stain on a Jewish cheek.
Thank you for your tears, Lord.
    They are, in a way,
    a proof of ownership.
    You own us
    because you love us,
    because you cry for us.

Go to the village opposite. You will find a donkey
there, as you enter it. Bring it to me. And if anyone
says anything to you, answer:'The Lord has need of it'.
Luke 19:30,31

I thought, Lord,
you would have done better
with someone else;
      older, perhaps,
      more settled,
      more fitted to the job.
I said: "I am a child,
      I do not know how to speak,
      I do not know how to carry you".
But all these words
      died on my lips
      when I heard your voice.
And knowing you needed me
      I trotted forward.

Jesus went into the temple . . . and overturned the tables
of the money changers and those who sold doves.
Matthew 21:12

You have a funny way of going to church, Lord.
I half expected you
       in cassock and stole,
       intoning old psalms
         and reverent, devout hymns.
But you came to upset all my tables, Lord,
all my settled habits of mind
         and assumptions about you,
            taken for granted over many years:
          these are overturned and put to flight.
And so, Lord,
         you who come to fill my life
         with good things and kind blessings,
         are welcomed also
            as an Emptier.

He took the bread and gave thanks, and broke it.
'This is my body'. Luke 22:19

All your life is here
in this plain bread we eat,
this ordinary meal we share.
There is no need,
now or later,
to change or be changed,
except with your love.
Here, in this ordinary life,
is all we ever need.

*Finally, when the mockery was over, they took off
the mantle and dressed him in his own clothes.*
Matthew 27:31

I wonder if the soldiers knew
                what they were doing, Lord.
For in stripping you,
and tearing off your robe,
they exposed more
          than a carpenter's back for beating.
They showed to the world
       more than one man's vulnerability.
       If only they had known it,
       they tore the curtain in the sanctuary as well,
       showing to the world
           not just your nakedness,
               but God's love.

So they came to a place called Golgotha.
Matthew 27:33

I don't think I've anything to be proud of, Lord.
We all betray you,
                one way or another;
or deny you, or run away.
Peter and Andrew,
and Thomas with his doubting,
only did what we do now.
They are our brothers,
                like us needing forgiveness:
and receiving your love.

Judas returned the thirty silver pieces
to the chief priests and elders. 'I have sinned. I have
brought an innocent man to his death'. Matthew 27:3, 4

Those who die by their own hand, Lord,
have a special place in your love.
You appeal to them with special marks of your affection.
And if, as now, they seem to betray you,
you share that death on another tree,
             and perhaps, their dereliction.
You appear to them first of all, in your resurrection,
that they may find, after the darkness,
             a new morning.

My God, my God, why have you forsaken me?
Matthew 27:46

You used to be in control of events, Lord,
but now events control you.
You are held fast by Roman rope
                and nails and wood.
You cannot speak
            except in sharp sentences of pain.
You cannot walk.
And you, who gave sight to the blind,
now need to see some purpose
            in your own life,
            your own death.

Father, into your hands . . . Luke 23:46

You don't seem to have changed much, Lord.
　　The doors were all closed when you first
　　　　　came to see us,
　　as they are now.
　　The doors of the synagogue sliding shut,
　　society itself forcing you out,
　　and our own hearts, above all,
　　still occupied with other things.
　　　　Yet, Lord,
　　　　　though we leave you outside
　　　　　in this place of dereliction,
　　　　　your life still speaks to us.
　　　　　As at Bethlehem, so now:
　　　　　"Behold, I stand at the door and knock".

*Now there stood by the cross of Jesus his mother
and her sister, Mary, the wife of Cleopas, and
Mary of Magdala.* John 19:25

It is strange how you express yourself, Lord:
    a whole life, expressed in three hours,
    a whole love, expressed in one death,
    thirty-three years crystallised
            in one moment of affection:
            "Father, for their sakes . . ."
And if it's not too late to say so, Lord,
thank you for coming,
though it seemed at the time
          a strange visit:
the hay and the crib
         to welcome you,
not much else.
And now at the end,
        wood and nails again to bid you goodbye.
Yet we, who can only offer
      the wood and straw of our own life
        are grateful
        because we know
        you will use us,
          if you will.

It is finished. John 19:30

It takes a long time to make a life, Lord.
So many ordinary days at Joseph's bench.
So many nails hammered in,
pieces of wood shaped to order.
And none of it,
      at the time,
      seeming to influence events,
      seeming to change
            the darkness of a hostile world.
   Yet in the end you did,
   leaving us not tables and chairs,
   but your own life, now accomplished.

In conclusion,
I have only this to add,
something I've been trying to say
for thirty-three years,
for thirty-three million years.
But only now,
in these three awkward hours,
do I seem to find the opportunity
of summing it all up.
In one word,
in one life,
in one death,
son, daughter,
I love you.

Joseph of Arimathea, being a disciple secretly,
begged Pilate that he might take away the body.
And Nicodemus came as well, who had first come
to Jesus by night. John 19:38,39

I came by night, Lord.
Not everyone is brave enough
to commit himself more openly.
And then, when it was night again,
    and the sun was setting
                on Friday afternoon,
                and on your life,
    I came with Joseph
    to ask your body of Pilate,
    to bury you.
    It was too late to do more,
    so I did what I could.
    And yet, Lord,
    we who serve you,
    shyly and with diffidence,
    also love you.
    And we who vote for you uncertainly
    will yet do better.

Pilate was surprised that he was already dead.
Mark 15:44

I think this was a small resurrection, Lord,
    a small light, shining in the dark,
    two shy men, asking for your body;
    coming to help you
                at the epilogue of your life
when it was too late
and they wished they had come earlier.
And all they could do was bury you.
Yet those who come to you
                in the darkest hour, Lord,
will find you in the morning.

They made the grave secure; sealed with a stone, and guarded. Matthew 27:66

When all hope is gone, Lord,
you are born.
When the darkness is complete,
you come.
When things are beyond hope,
in the territory of utter despair,
we find you.
>You roll back the stone
>and are there to greet us.

*Mary of Magdala, Mary the mother of James, and
Salome brought sweet spices to anoint him. Very early on
the Sunday morning they came to the tomb.* Mark 16:1

I look for you in the wrong places:
bringing my flowers to recreate old memories,
my ointment to rub in old situations,
                    old friendships.
And yet, Lord,
          you give me something better
          than an old life repeated:
          you give me a new life in my own.

He gave them his greeting. Matthew 28:10

I don't know what you said, Lord,
the exact words you used.
Perhaps it was only 'shalom',
      your usual greeting.
But to us, then, standing in the garden,
      broken and utterly alone,
        it was a hand on our shoulder,
        and new breath in our lungs.
        "Peace", you said, and still say:
          "Do not be afraid".

*Go quickly and tell his disciples he is risen
from the dead.* Matthew 28:7

This has been a tough assignment, Lord,
and still we have hardly begun,
conveying your love to people in all generations,
 all circumstances of life,
 on different continents.
 Yet however great the distance
 that separates you from us,
 we are still, as Peter was,
 your brothers,
 your disciples.

The same day two of them were on their way to Emmaus . . .
As they talked and discussed it with one another, Jesus himself
came and walked with them. But something stopped them
knowing who he was. Luke 24:13-16

When two people walk
on any journey,
when two people travel, Lord
a long path together,
there comes a time,
not easy to pinpoint,
when all their onward journeying
bears fruit.
And they find
not two,
but a third person
travelling their journey
with them.

*That night they went fishing and toiled all night,
catching nothing. When daybreak came, Jesus himself
stood on the shore, though they did not know it was
him. "Friends", he cried, "have you caught anything?"
Then he said: "Throw your net the other side of
the boat". And they did so, bringing in so great a catch
that the net began to break.* John 21:3-6

One gets discouraged, Lord,
when you've gone on as long as I have,
doing your best with no result.
I have tried every throw of the net,
      everything I am capable of.
      But it is now, Lord,
         after a lifetime's failure,
         that you yourself call to me;
         and at your word
         I let down the net.

Jesus stood on the shore. John 21:4

I know it's a new day, Lord,
but the lessons of the night
        do count for something.
        Surely you can see that.
        Yet, if you tell me to,
        I will obey.
        Silly as it sounds,
        and against all my experience,
        I turn round
            and throw down the net
            from the other side of my life.

Simon, son of John, do you love me?
John 21:15

Lord, you know how I feel about you.
   I do not need to exaggerate
      or make extravagant claims;
      or to compare myself with others,
      some of whom will do better,
      some, it may be, even worse.
      But I say that I love you
         as well as I can.
         I say that I am your friend.

Peter was sad when Jesus asked him the third time:
'Do you love me?' He replied: 'Lord, you know everything'.
John 21:17

It is not easy repeating oneself, Lord,
saying: 'I love you,
            and I will follow you'
            for the second and third,
            for the three hundredth time.
            Yet we do it,
            as well as we can.
            As a young man or woman, first,
            more easily.
            Then, when we are older
            and tied down to the world and life
            by a thousand little cords,
            we say again the old words,
            'Lord, you know that I am your friend'.
            And though we say it with awkwardness,
            with rheumatism in our limbs,
            and tiredness and lost opportunities
                    in our hearts,
            still you hear us, and receive us.
                    And lead us on.

If it is my will that he remain until I come,
what is that to you? John 21:22

Your servant, John,
    lived so long, Lord,
    they thought he would never die,
    but live to see your return.
    And perhaps he did not die, Lord,
    but is still here
       in your church,
          silently waiting.
          Perhaps your church is,
             in a way,
             John himself,
             still waiting, though older,
             a sign to all the world
             that you will come again;
          that peace and justice
             shall at last
        triumph on earth.

I will go before you into Galilee. Matthew 26:32

You said you would see us in Galilee, Lord,
not in some rare religious experience
available only to a few,
but in our old lives,
    our old familiar places,
    fishing nets often mended,
        and a well-known coast.
    Here you would appear to us
        and see us regularly,
till at last we knew what you had always told us:
that you are with us always.

As he blessed them he was parted from them.
Luke 24:51

The last picture we have of you, Lord,
    is perhaps the best,
    perhaps the most typical,
    and we shall always remember it.
    It is how you lived,
    it is how you died,
    hands raised up to bless us,
    your thirty years on earth complete
    as you make your last journey
    to dwell in our hearts for ever.
    For as you lived,
        healing the sick, blessing the poor,
    so are you taken from us,
    blessing us as you return to the Father.
    You do not say good-bye.
    Only: "I am with you always,
             to the end of time".

Go, tell all nations. Matthew 28:.19

Lord, you are always with us.
No weakness of ours can keep you away,
     no besetting sin.
     In all seasons,
          and at all times,
          you are with us,
               till we meet again.

And the light shone in the darkness,
and the darkness did not put it out.
John 1:5

It is strange, Lord,
the effect of a candle:
so trivial a thing,
so small a piece of wax.
And yet I light it,
and for a little space
the darkness
is driven back,
so that the world itself
is lighter
—because of my candle,
because of one good deed,
because of one life.